# Cactus
# Blossoms

By Alexis Marie

ISBN: 9781719979948

Imprint: Independently Published

As you embark on your journey, be sure to take care of yourself. There are points of view included in this book that were written when I was in a dark state of mind and may be harmful to your mental health if read in the wrong state of mind. PLEASE TAKE CARE OF YOURSELF. Included context includes writing about suicide, rape, addiction, self-harm, abuse, etc. If you are feeling alone, insignificant or helpless, please reach out to your support system. Your support system is so much bigger than you think!

or call 1-800-273-8255.

# The
# Sun

My soul is drained from the people

I surround

myself with,

from the situations I put my energy

towards solving.

Too sick and tired

to continue to be sick and tired,

But too busy
to do anything about it.

This is my life.

The air I fill my lungs with has sickened me for months now.

Stale,

Repetitive,

Never ending and always stagnant.

To whoever is listening,

*please send something to light up my world.*

I cannot do this anymore.

At the same place

at the same time every day.

Round and round they go,

I bet they have more fun than I do.


*-clock hands*

Lackluster.

My days are knitted together

with needles of comfort

and yarn of stability.

I am too

self-loathing for that.

Love at first sight doesn't exist...

But my

*God*

You make a good case.

I have never seen someone so
effortlessly stop time.


*-first impressions*

As he drifted by,

he was so cool,

That the sun could pull up a chair,

sit down at the table next to him and introduce itself.

They'd shake hands and exchange blinding smiles,

But his palms would never break a sweat.

Like the man on the cover of a GQ magazine,

who unknowingly mastered the skill over the years,

He had mastered the art of captivation.


*-you and Gatsby*

Behind the bartender at 1:46 am,

Through the double vodkas

and the night sky,

you remind me,

what a light can do

to a dark room.

His eyes,

held the whole universe in them.

They had taken me so off guard,

I missed my chance.

It was gone and

so was my breath.

Conversations half minded,

Looking, but not seeing.

I am constantly searching for you

in every pair of eyes

and in every passing pair of shoes.

Every accidental bump of the elbow,

I hope to see your eyes

staring back at me when I apologize.

I will see you again.

The universe wants me to,

I can feel it.

And who am I to argue with the universe?

There it is again,

Something so magical and full of
wonder.

Let me take a closer look.

I'll leave my breath behind,

I won't need it, anyways.

As a lamb who delights

in the seduction of wolves,

I can tell you first hand...

the risk of the wolf,

is the seduction of the lamb.

You look at me like I have made great
accomplishments,

As though my feet touching the ground
you stand upon, is enough for you.


My sweet love,

*Tell me,*


What do you see that makes you look at
me like I am the person I have only ever
aspired to be?

You smell like a peaceful soul

and a good night sleep.

Like sage sent from the earth

to cleanse my soul

of all the filthy fingerprints from past
ghosts.

Come closer;

stay with me.

They looked at us

as if they knew

we didn't belong together.

But like they understood.


*-change minds with me*

In between

Head over heels and faceplanted,

is where you can find me.

Smack dab

in the middle of Smitten and blindsided;

after lust

and just in front of the sign that says

*Completely Fucked.*

She flutters so loud when she knows
you're near;

so loud my logic can't be heard.

She wants to break free and meet you;

that overexcited butterfly.

When I'm next to you,

she's most fussy,

she bangs her clumsy wings

against my empty chest.

She bangs, and bangs, and bangs

while the echoes ring in my ears.

I cannot think of anything else,

I'm sure you can hear her too.

I'm know she wants to meet you;

that noisy little butterfly.

Maybe one day I'll let her.

I'll rip her from my chest

and place her in your hands.

You will finally know

what's making all that noise

and how distracting she really is.

I yearn to watch

the demons dance

between our eyes.

How beautiful a performance

they would create together;

with dancing fingers and pounding hearts.

The songs you let slip out

will be the most

sensational symphonies

I've ever heard.

Let our demons dance, baby.

Make music with me.

His inner magnetism
demanded such harsh attention.
He was with me everywhere,
even when he wasn't.

You can tell by looking at me,

I have spent many days

under the love spell of the sun.

She marks me as her territory,

unapologetically,

with the sand colored lipstick,

she leaves on my warm skin.

Her kisses leave me breathless and
sweaty,

but she is the biggest consistency in my
life.

You had a different lover.

The glimmer of your iced eyes

had spent months

under the beckoning call of the moon.

Your skin,

fragile to the caress of anything warmer
than your own hands,

was a delicacy.

People have searched

for that type of softness for years....

in eyes,

in smiles...

in souls of the innocent,

And here it is, all 6 feet of it.

I would leave the sun every day,

betray her at no mercy,

make my indiscretions public

so all of the other suns knew,

just to spend one night

under the moon with you.

To be able to turn raindrops into floods,

Moans into thunderstorms,

And shutters into earthquakes,

 you must be the disaster my world needs.

Watch me bloom.

Watch as I build myself up

after you have consumed my every fiber
in the storm.

Destruction is a form of creation.

I'm begging you my sweet love,

*destroy me.*

His voice

was the fire my shivering bones sat in front of. Hands stretched out with goose bump covered skin, just his words were enough to wrap me in warmth and caress me back to life.

Eyes,

the unexplored, intriguing and mesmerizing deep green sea. I could lose my way within a split second and be forced to accept the strength of water; knowing the waves are too powerful for me to defeat.

His hands

ripped through my hair like the wind on the freeway. It was the kind of mess only he and a rolled down window could leave behind.

The taste of his neck

breathed air into my lungs, but the taste of his shoulders breathed life. I'd let my only source of oxygen be his skin if it was okay with him.

*-my worlds elements*

You could paint a masterpiece on my skin,

Let's give it a try.

I've got plenty of red shoved into this heart of mine.

You've got the perfect shade of green lingering in those eyes.

You always tell me how beautiful bright colors look on my tan skin.

 Let me show you what we can do together.

Knowing how particular he can be is my favorite part.

He has chosen me.

I have passed tangible standards and finally loved myself so hard,

I can be considered good enough.


*-he won't love you until you learn to love yourself*

There is so much trouble

in my eyes I cannot hide from you.

Is that why you look at me like that,

You just need to figure it all out?

Peel back the layers

and find whatever there is to find?

Yes,

you're right.

My baggage is heavy.

I have been carrying it for years,

but I am doing just fine on my own.

Thank you for offering.

Let me love the parts of you,

that you don't know exist.

I'll find each

nook

and cranny

and crevice

you hide from the world.

No corner could ever be too dark.

I'll never shy away,

never blink

or shutter.

No part of you

could ever be too much.

I can be the daydream that gets you out
of bed,

The honey on your toast,

Or your first cup of coffee at 5:15 am.

A warm pick me up

cradled between your hands,

as you crave the one thing

that will get you through your morning.

I want to be the reason

you look forward to a new day.

My biggest accomplishment
of the day is sharing a table with him
and being able to breathe the same air.
But my favorite part
is when he tilts his head to the side
and asks me to repeat myself
a little louder.
He says
it is too loud to hear my words
and places his hand on my leg.
It's one of his most common habits.
Maybe he uses it as an excuse
to be closer to me,
or maybe he thinks the air
smells a little sweeter
when we're next to each other,
like I do.
Maybe we're in sync,

like the stars and the night time

or the ocean and the moon.

After all,

the night without the stars

would be a dark travesty

and the ocean without the moon

would just be a puddle.

Happiness makes people glow, you
know?

If I could spend every evening

watching sunsets with you,

I'd be glowing with beauty.

You'd make me so bright,

the sun couldn't bear to keep staring.

She'd bow to her knees every night

knowing I had outshined her.

*-sunsets*

I have never taken a shot this strong.

Please have mercy on me,

Loving this hard,

loving this free,

is my absolute biggest fear.

Deep

Between

my

legs

is

my

love

for

you.

Go

explore,

go

find

it.

My only dream

is to bottle up his kisses

and become a billionaire.

We'll sell so many to people

just like me,

there will be no hurt left in the world.

If we could just bottle up

the happiness he brings,

the world would be at peace.

We'd forget about our troubles and past,

Find peace and overdue happiness.

If I could just bottle up his kisses,

We'd make this world

the type of beautiful we all deserve.

If you ever need someone

to walk across the ocean

and drown for you,

I'm a horrible swimmer.

I'll give you the road map you need.

I'll lead you around every curve,

every corner.

*Watch my fingers.*

I'll show you how to navigate the
downpours

and the earthquakes

as if you were born

with the map

in your head.

Cabernet,

golden hour,

and cotton candy skies.


*-he's my happy hour*

Words are so clumsy around you.

Who needs them anyways?

Come with me.

We can find the perfect place

to root our flowers together.

We can pick the perfect spot

 in the garden to plant them,

So they can get just the right amount of sun.

We can water them together

or take turns if you'd like.

We'll spend our days

picking out our favorite clouds as they pass by

or sipping sweet tea

on the wrap around porch

as we watch the bees pollinate.

Let's relish in how fresh they smell,

knowing together,

we gave this garden to the world.

You curve your tongue

with the vulnerability of an escape plan.

I can feel it

as you drag yourself in circles

and swallow all my fears.

Your tongue

is my favorite part of you.

Being next to him didn't make me

want to write poetry,

he made me want to live it.

*My sweet love,*
You are the morning breath
and the evening sigh.
I have wandered
from corner to corner
and stumbled every step.
My hands and knees
may be a little bruised,
but it was worth it.
You are my other half,
you are my home.

I'm not saying

I'm hard to love.

I'm saying

this is going to take

a lot of patience.

Like

a

shadow

to

the

L I G H T

I'll

be

your

S L A V E

without

a

second

thought.

Starting my day off

with candied bacon

and mimosas

would always

be second best

to bed head

and his

morning smile.

How beautiful

to have found

someone who admired my curves

with the same passion

as he admires my thoughts.

Undress me,

like you have my mind.

Asking what he was craving for dinner,
I turned my head towards the window
as my eyes rolled in the back of my head
without a second thought.

*Vanilla ice cream to go with your
caramel skin.*

How was I supposed to argue with that?

Do you know how hard it is,

to ignore the

purple polka dot umbrella

shoved in his passenger side door?

My truth

will ruin this moment

and this moment

may be all we have.


*-unbroken silence*

You must be good

at making the piano tingle, too.

Play for me,

I'll play for you.

How could one person

make me so excited

to share a meal and a shower?

How could one person

make me so happy

to be alive?

The 4:30 am sound of the ceiling fan

is my favorite part of my day.

When I roll over and

see you snoring so peacefully,

you're sweeter than white wine.

My favorite pastime

is counting the seconds until you wake,

when I can kiss your cheeks

and run my hands through your hair.

How lucky am I,

to have a morning

full of so much fresh air.

I am not very good

at stopping myself

when I know it's wrong...

I should work on that.

His hands don't remind me

of my fathers.

They're smooth, soft. Caressing my
cheeks

with these long fingers attached to them,

he reaches in my soul

and opens his eyes to exactly what I
need.

He whispers how proud of me he is

as he cradles my face between his palms.

His hands move steadily,

confidently.

There is peace in them,

His hands

are not like my fathers at all.

I could watch another's hand

hang the moon,

but I'd still believe you

if you told me

you were responsible

for lighting up my darkness.

There is not a single thing
I want more in this moment
then to take a chance on you.
Just be with me.
Who cares about the rest?
We'll figure it out.

The way you look at me

when I touch you,

there's no way

she can do that for you

or you wouldn't be here.

Let me fill you up

with the love she can't.

I can show you what it's like

to live again.

He grew flowers in the darkest corners,

of the deepest caves.

How was I supposed to write about
anything else?

Today I watched a bee drown in its own honey,

That's when I understood the mess I had just made.

I was the bee that had only myself to blame.

We created this beautiful enigma for the world to enjoy

And it drowned me before I got to enjoy it.


*-I was supposed to write a ten word story (50 word story*

# The Thorns

Of all the shadows on my bedroom wall,

How could the scariest one

have been him this whole time,

When not a single ounce of ill intention

lingered in his five am eyes.

*In my 44 years,*

*you are the first thing*

*I have ever done for myself.*


*-things he says to justify me staying his*
*second choice*

The line separating

destroyed and not,

is between the secrets

you let spew through the air.

How fucking heartbreaking.

Come hell or high water,

as your God as my witness,

I will burn your world to the ground

and use the flames

to light my own damn sky.

They always knew what they needed to
do.

They needed to rip themselves apart

at the seams

and never wander back.

They knew they belonged apart

for the good of the world.


*-the coasts*

Every blanket

I attempted to crochet

was woven together

with strings of my goose bump covered
skin,

while using a needle

made of my fragile and breaking bones.

How dare you handle my soul with such
care.

Cradle it.

Examine it.

Poke and prod,

just to leave me in the cold

without so much as

a blanket to keep myself warm.

He knocked so gently

but demanding.

Eyes starving,

ravenous.

And a smile perfectly inviting...

How was I not supposed to let him in.


*-it was the way he looked at me*

My father always hollered so loud,

*'This is for your own good,*
*I do this because I love you.*
*I know what's best for you.'*

And now here I am
stuck on a motel floor
because my boyfriend of 7 months
has finally yelled so loud
I think my heart has shattered.
I'm beginning to think
being loved isn't for me.

I have lied to my mother
about my bruises,
I have lied to my father
about my tears,
but most importantly,
I have lied to myself
about my happiness.

My emotions
trumped logic
for you.
I am a fool.

Liberation comes with a cost.

I have missed

being the first one to tell you

happy birthday

and I have missed surprising you

at your new job

with celebration coffee.

I'll never know

if your basil grew

after you tried placing it

closer to the window,

In the name of liberation.

I have been standing under the shower water

For far too long,

because my lukewarm skin

Is the closest thing I can find to your arms

wrapped around me.

I have missed so much in the name

of independence.

*-liberated, lonely and lukewarm*

He carried me in his hands

like a bowl of overflowing water.

He skipped merrily along,

as parts of me sloshed around,

and landed on the floor behind him.

Then he lost his temper

when he realized I was only half full,

expecting me to know

where all the water had gone.

Folded hands and a closed heart,

With bruised knees

and a heart heavier

than an anchor at sea.

I am sentenced to a life

of kneeling before

a god I don't believe in

just in the hopes

of seeing you again.

I could have held it behind my back,

asked you to close your eyes

and put your hands out.

Or

maybe wrapped up

in beautiful gold and white paper

with a giant bow on top,

Or

in newspaper and scotch tape,

if you prefer.

I would have given you my heart

anyway you wanted it.

There is magic in the destruction you
left.

I cannot find it,

but sorting through the debris

I feel it...

A second chance,

A fresh start

A new sense of self-worth.

There is still hope.

Maybe between your silver tongue

and your transparent promises,

there is the magic

of who I am meant

to rebuild myself as.

I just need look harder.

I have long been starving

and homesick

for a place

that hasn't existed.

And the worst part

about being homeless,

is how easy it is

to confuse people with homes.

How foolish of me to create a home

inside the soul

of such a ruthless man.

Someone who thrives

off destruction

and feeds on misplaced trust.

I tried to build

inside a man

who lacks

Compassion,

Empathy,

And self-awareness.

How foolish of me.


*-Daisy warned me*

I am not a priority of yours


And I am tired


Of telling myself


I am.

He only wanted me

to fill up the empty spaces

that surrounded him.

I was stuck on the freeway

in rush hour traffic,

during a thunderstorm

and

*I still chose him.*

My biggest reminder

that time is a privilege

and the only thing

that makes me wish

things were different.


*-you*

Have you ever surrounded yourself with

people who pound the emotion out of you?

People who leave you a little more callus

then ask why you have no heart?

Like they forget it's beating in their own hand.

Maybe they don't forget,

Maybe they know it's there the whole time

and they just choose to be that cruel.

I wish I could delight in power that way.

There are too many
unwelcomed parasites
that gnawed away at my soul
late at night.
All are named after you.

We were just two runaways

sprinting away from the same place,

who tripped over each other's shoelaces

before we got where we were going.

It doesn't matter

that I was the moon and you the ocean.

They never touched after all,

One was just in control over the other.


 *-maybe they ended up as strangers
because they made the same choices as
us*

I have spent my fair share of days

locked away in darkness,

And after all that

I would always choose

the color of my blood

over

the color of darkness

any day.

Solo PBR

and bar snacks

ran a truck

through my heart.

His ghost follows me

closer than my own shadow;

it's stronger than the tequila

he begged to lick from my stomach.

His ghost lurks

in the seldom quiet

of a downtown bar

at three pm begging

to be filled with his laughter.

How can I cling to someone

who has been a ghost

longer than he has been a person?

The look in his eyes

was simply a soul

who was just as lost as I was.


-he won't love you until you love yourself

The dust is settled,

It's easier this way.


*-I hate sneezing*

Do you remember

how ravenous you used to look at me?

How the only cheap thrill I needed

was that stupid smile you'd give me

at the beginning of each visit.

It was like all those metaphors

about suns and moons and fire and
thunder

only ever existed

in the space between us.

No one

has ever looked at me like you have,

I don't want them to either,

I want that place to be yours

forever.

I want to write

and write

and write

until my heart

is relieved of all this pain

and my mind is silent.

But

My words

...

...

...

...

they won't come out.

...

...

...

My heart is too sad

to put letters together nicely.

*-when you left I couldn't even write
about it*

I carried him in the bags

under my eyes

and in between my frown lines.

His name was written on my t-shirt

in the same font EDC is written in

and if he was as easy to lose

as those 7 pounds,

maybe I wouldn't have been so
distracted

the last few weeks.

Whether you want the love or not,

your oxygen will be a little less pure

when it's over.

A struggle to breathe.

That's what we get

for thinking we deserve

love in the first place.

We are too narcissistic for this world.

I know,

The karma

is written all over me.


-*Humans*

He took me to the ocean

to drown me

when he couldn't keep his secrets
anymore.

It was my fault the water was rising,

It was my fault his devotion

was being questioned.


*It was always going to be my fault.*


The waves were sent to destroy his
house

and leave him left with nothing

but destroyed photos

and a soggy, cold and empty bed,

because of me.


*-I have a theory he was picturing himself*
*when he held my head under water*

I could still feel the way

he shook his leg

under our favorite tucked away table.

I can see it out of the corner of my eye

if I don't focus too hard.

I can hear myself making sure he's okay,

asking if he's stressed.

I can hear my giggle

as he apologizes and tells me,

*Your eyes still make me nervous
sometimes.*

I miss his voice.

I miss my giggle.

I miss the shaking table.

I miss him so much.

How knotted yarn made of insecurity

and self-loathing can be.

All tangled up in a ball

as I fidget my fingers through the knots,

I no longer know

how long I have been sitting here.

What a black hole I've been devoured
into,

How cruel an influence

distance has on an idle mind.

I begged him to have mercy

But he destroyed me

without a single regret for his soul.


*-A frightening type of careless*

How many sins

are wrapped between

those perfectly straight teeth of his?

How many lies

has he managed to let slither

through his lips and destroy worlds?

And how is it possible

that all his sins just sparkle,

lighting up the darkest corners

of the deepest caves?

He may be the closest thing to a monster

I have ever met.

Knowing the moon kept watch over you,

made it a little less painful.

She watched you

the way I wished I could.

She will keep you safe,

I trust her.

She makes me feel peaceful,

like my soul can rest for a second.

The moon is the only thing

that makes me feel better.

His fingertips set fires,

but fires destroy.

Fires leave only ashes.


*-my burned down body*

How could I

deem him a monster,

when I know

he was only

being human?

Never again will we be anything.

We have run out of chances

And for that my heart breaks.


*-1:37 am bathroom thoughts*

How dare you

make

a heartbroken poet

out of me.

When we realized how giant

our sparks were getting,

we suffocated them

instead of letting them steal

more pieces of ourselves.


-*we've been here before (self-*
*preservation)*

The worst part of this whole thing?

He still gets to walk the earth

with that flawless face.

He'll drift by like he does

and leave humanity breathless.

She won't know how tainted his soul is

or how selfish he chooses to be.

His soul does not deserve its facility.


*-this one makes me angry when I read it*
*out loud*

How calming to know

He isn't the last one

to leave his nasty fingerprints all over
me.

No longer will he linger

like winter snow long after its destroyed

springs flowers.


*-it was cold last night, I hope his garden
died*

When I walked away

from the tofu version of him,

I realized I would have done anything

just to have one more taste.


*-tofu is disgusting (not really, but he was.)*

You are not the cause of my illness

You are a symptom.

How dare you call yourself my lover

and be so narcissistic.


I am not the cause of your illness

I am a symptom.

How dare I call myself your lover

and be so narcissistic.


*-abusive relationships*

A man at the grocery store

walked by me today

and that was the first time

I had smelled it since.

I hope she broke the cologne bottle

over your head when she found out.

I don't want to talk about it,

Only because

people are tired of hearing it.

I just can't make them understand.

*What did you do to your hair?!*

he said as eight months sat in front of us

*I almost didn't even recognize you!*

*-good*

A snake

can only

strike if

you trust

it enough

to turn

your back

on it.


*-There are no rules in love or war*

Somehow,

I've ended up

with another broken

wine glass.


*-things don't just fall, someone must
push them*

I'm sorry for suction cupping to you

so quickly,

I just missed you so much.

I didn't want to think

about a second without you.

Easier than remembering to blink,

And more thrilling than anything

I have ever been a part of.

Nostalgia can be a black hole at this
hour,

but I am tired of fighting it.

I loved you and I am not ashamed of it.

Falling for you was the easiest thing

I have ever done.

I told him I'd love him

whole heartedly,

No matter what

he gave back.

I take it back,

I take it all back.

It

is three am

and I am happy

we are strangers.

These days I forget

we live in the same world.

My day is eaten right up,

Second by second,

Minute by minute.

There are responsibilities to be taken
care of.

But

When I catch a moment of silence

in between songs on the radio

or waiting for my coffee,

I remember,

There was a day our paths crossed

out of pure destiny.

The whole universe lined up for that
second;

The whole universe believed in us

And you let her down.

Being fully aware

of your existence is

torture.

Soft

Brutal

And constant

Torture.

If you can sleep at night

knowing what you did,

then I don't want your love,

anyways.

*-I hope she asks why there are bags
under your eyes*

My puddle of tears is bigger

Than the puddle of spilled milk

That has sat there for 11 months.


*-lactose intolerant*

The only sound sweeter

than you begging for mercy,

was the sound of the door slamming

to make it stop.

The scariest part about monsters,

is that they are

exclusively human.

They can love and be loved,

Laugh and cry.

They hide in plain sight

just waiting for people like you or me,

People who are a little hurt and a little
lost.

Taking joy in hiding behind

perfectly straight smiles

and beautiful compliments.

When you hug them,

they'll smell familiar,

Like something your soul

has yearned for in every passed life.

Monsters can be so tricky

And the irony of it all?

That's what makes me

so curious about them.


*-how could I be so stupid*

# The Drought

How vile a core

he must have,

to treat others

with such callus.

I remember telling myself

he was just looking for the pieces of me

he couldn't find at first glance.

So,

he pushed and pushed and pushed,

Until my insides

were vomited on the floor

in front of him.

And when he realized

he couldn't find what he was looking for,

he swung

and swung

and swung

at the reflection of himself in my eyes.

He kept me there until he pummeled

every bit of himself out.

He couldn't stand the sight of him,

as much as I couldn't.

Searching for your highs

will only ruin your highs.


*-trying too hard to forget*

If you don't want to sink,

you'll learn how to swim

*-self swimming life jacket*

My father

was busy

the day

I arrived,

My father

was busy

the day

I departed.


-two different fathers disappointed in two
different ways

My world is lit

with stars

I can play connect the dots with.

They create a black coffin,

with one tiny hole to see out of

and a promise of how temporary time is.

So many of those dots

have collapsed and reformed.

How silly of me

to think this is important,

When my coffin

is destroying and recreating itself

every night, too.


*-stars collapse, why can't I?*

You showed us all

Clear as day.

You showed us what was happening
inside,

and no one did a thing about it.

So,

you festered and rotted and reeked

until the smell got so bad

James had to break down the door.

You showed us every day

what a mess you were

and now you're not here

for me to help you clean up.

Instead It's just all of us...

Staring blankly into the abyss,

pretending there were no warning signs.

All of us,

the people who said they loved you,

All of us,

the ones who didn't do a damn thing
about it

when you were screaming

at the top of your lungs.

*-I'm to blame too*

I gagged at the stench of your space

as I collapsed on the floor.

If this is what the outside smelled like,

*You poor soul,*

What was the inside like?

*Cleanliness is next to godliness*

My father would always say.

That's why the clouds

are always so white

after the rainstorm,

The angels

are hanging their sheets out to dry.

What a mess you must have made up there,

 for the clouds to still be so grey

after they've already been washed.


*-You were always a little messy*

In the brown moving box

farthest in the back of my mind.

The one labeled

**DO NOT OPEN,**

That is where you live.

My saving grace

is my demise

and if my demise is my legacy,

know I loved every second.


*-caffeine, nicotine and cocaine*

Burning too brightly

and burning bridges...

Well,

those must be the same thing.


-*a flame is a flame*

We are where we are,

because when she looked at me,

it was the first time she ever saw

her reflection

in anything other than the mirror.


-*she must not like what she sees*

I just wanted to be

the love of your life.


*-To my parents*

When I realized,

my tears alone

could turn puddles

into lakes

and lakes into oceans,

I finally understood

what they meant

when they said

*manmade.*

Maybe the cosmos

only see violence

as an option,

because it's the only method

that yields universes.

I cannot live my life without you

pounding in my head

with your heavy iron fist.

Spending your days painting black stars

in my eyeballs

and clumsily pulling on strings

like you forgot your mother told you

not to touch things

that don't belong to you.

Your talon nails

have tried to pierce my skin

so many times this week,

it's hard to focus on anything else

And when you decide

to make yourself a guest here,

my muscles must work twice as hard.

I am trying to live a life

fit for the person I want to be

And you are making my body ache.

You are not welcome here.

*-IF I EVER PHYSICALLY MEET DEPRESSION I'LL MURDER IT.*

Just because you did not see the fire,

doesn't mean it was not here.

Just because your head was turned,

and your eyes were closed,

doesn't mean the destruction

did not happen.

If a flower

loses its life over him,

Justice is nothing more

than a tale

told for weak people to cling to.


*-don't cut flowers when he dies, he's not*
*worth another life*

My own feelings

terrify me enough

to send me into hiding.

How am I supposed to face

anything else?

I find it strange,

I can recognize

a demon's claws when

they drag across my skin

without ever having laid eyes on them.

Bursting through the old moving box

I had stuffed them in,

Claws first,

The feeling of my flesh being ripped
open

is an easily recognizable one.

I have put up a good fight,

I will win the war,

 I hope.

But the battle of the night is lost.

I may be bloody and weak,

but the game my demons are playing will

start over tomorrow

and I will get a chance to even the score.

To prove to myself and everyone around
me

why I belong here.

I will get the chance

to see the sun rise

and set

and when I feel my demons

 release their fingers from my wrist

without leaving a mark,

I'll know

it was because of my own strength

my skin has not been torn through.

When they crawl back into

the old brown stingy smelling box,

They'll file their talons.

Sharpening them into the daggers

that pain me in such a recognizable way.

Then I will fall

asleep,

Safe,

Exhausted,

Drained.

Unsure if I can muster up

the strength to go through

the same battle again tomorrow.


But the victory of my day

will always inspire my fight

to see the sun rise.

To see the way the clouds wave in the
air,

the way they do

when talon clawed hands

wave a white surrender flag.

My victories are what keep me fighting

And fight I will.


*-I belong here, they don't*

Slithering into

 my 16 hour long dreams,

he has left my mind

exhausted.

How much longer

can I keep running

from such an insidious man

before my legs

simply

give out?

How much
more blood can I spew
before the people around me realize,
There is nothing left
But a completely drained
and lifeless
skeleton?

Does the word

*rape*

mean

rape

if I didn't say no?

Does the word

*consent*

mean

consent

if I didn't say yes?

Is it wrong for me

to label him a rapist knowing

I was too scared to say no?


*-no more bruises*

*I'm not stopping,*

he hissed.

*I have to keep going,*

*I can't start a car and not go anywhere.*

*-that's how he explained it to my 13-year-old self*

How many secrets do you think could hide in a shadow? That's the safest place to keep them, you know? I used to think shadows cast by trees were put there specifically to cover up the things we didn't want other people to see in the light. It was always so odd to me, there are so many people in this world, each with two eyes, and so many unrecognized injustices. The amount of sin that cannot recognize the light of day is not finite. It is eternal, it is constant, never ending. Always in sight but hidden, there are horrific and brutal things that your god himself cannot forgive when kingdom come. Things that live in the shadows, made by trees, planted by hands of the people you surround yourself with. The shadows are their safest place, not scrutinized and free of judgment.

When I was younger my mother used to tell me to go play in the woods. Looking back, that's where we kept secrets best. I used to look around and try to count the trees and their shadows.

I liked trying to calculate how many secrets you could fit into its shadow based on how wide or how tall the trees were...how many people could get away with whatever they wanted to if no one ever saw, if they were saved by the darkness?

After all my calculations, I realized there is bad in this world. There is evil. There is sinister. The small town my mother was so convinced had been the right choice was covered in trees.

I know I have

a lot

to be happy about

in my beautiful life,

But

I don't feel that way.

We can't possibly hear the same screams.

*-how much louder until you hear too*

- The multiverse
- Time isn't real
- Nothing is stopping me from going to the airport, getting on a plane and changing my name
- I am a spec on a floating piece of sand
- The multiverse

*-things I tell myself when it's all too much*

Killing myself would be stupid,

But it would feel so good.

Like the last shot

at 2 am

on a Wednesday night downtown.

It's one of those impulses

you get when driving 87

down the freeway

knowing it would only take

.2 seconds

to jerk your arm to the right

and send yourself flying in circles

through the air.

Or

when you stand on your balcony

in the silence of the night

and think about

how fast you could accidentally jump

from the third floor.

Killing myself

would be worth the adrenaline thrill,

but when it was over,

 I'd never have the chance to have
another.

 Plus,

people move on so quickly.

Monday,

there would be a therapist

for everyone to talk to at work and

Tuesday

everyone would be out for Taco
Tuesday.

If I kill myself,

my legacy

will only be half of what it's meant to be.

Dying is just as pointless as living.

And living is just as pointless as dying.

Wanderlust

just means

lost

after a while.

He follows me

to the darkest corners

of my mind,

like I'm not allowed to forget

the damage he's done.

Like I must

constantly envision

the way he slammed my neck

into the pavement.

His hissing

gives instructions in a tone

I thought only a god could use.

I must constantly be reminded

of how it felt to gasp

for air as he collapsed on top of me.

He is everywhere.

I can no longer stand

in the same space as him.

If he is here,

I am not.


*-lights on but no one's home*

If I could destroy myself

without repercussions,

I would.

If my demons could rip through my skin

without leaving a scar,

I would let them.

I wish

I could let them escape

without the world knowing

they were there in the first place.


-*demons who won't shut up (I have an
image to protect)*

My nightmares are nightmares,
because my truth
doesn't line up with the logic
of the world around me.

Wanting to die

isn't hostile

Or insecure

And it isn't selfish.

Wanting to die

is a peaceful solution to reset my soul.

It is emptiness fulfilled

as I become

a perpetual inhabitant

of the absolute darkness.

How dare you tell me it's selfish.

It isn't.

It's selfish of you to see me

in so much pain

and not do

a damn thing about it.


*-how much more do you think I can handle*

Here I am

writing suicide letters

and leaving my body

imprinted in the mattress.

I can't be left alone,

because alone is scary.

Alone is too dark,

too numb,

it's too heavy.

Every sharp object I see

magnets itself to my flesh

and I haven't slept in three days,

because I can no longer

stand the nightmares.


Here you are

busting through my bedroom door,

destroying my fight

with a sentence as simple as,

*My cousin Amy had anorexia once, but it was just a phase. You'll outgrow this too, it's just a phase; we have to let it run its course.*

So here I am,

helpless.

This phase is taking too long.

I'm not Amy.

What if I don't outgrow this?

What if this beats me before I beat it?

What if its course

is longer than I can take?

How am I

supposed to move passed this,

when I ask for help

and get told to wait it out?

What am I supposed to do

with all this sadness?

I have nowhere left to put it.

It's overflowing out of my eyes

and filling up my room.

I'm going to drown in here.

I'm going to drown in my own sadness.

My mind

has never been so numb.

If my chest

didn't rise and fall without instinct,

my soul would have left by now.

Holding your heart in your hands

for the world to see can be draining.

My heart can get really heavy sometimes,

I think that's why I'm always so sore.

My body is such a fighter

to have handled a heart so heavy,

full of watered down trust

and morning black coffee.

My hands become so exhausted,

they throw their own fits.

They get sore,

they get tired of aching,

Tired of carrying a load they didn't ask
for.

So frustrated and drained,

they can be a little too destructive.

They'll use their last bit of strength

to lash out,

But they don't mean it.

They're just exhausted

and know this can't last much longer.

My heart can get

really

heavy.

It gets so heavy,

sometimes my hands

just

give up.

*slice

-shit

This is all a bad dream.

Go home.


*-Lexy with a Y*

If your tears could sew me up,

we wouldn't have to go to the hospital
again.

We can use your tears as the stitches

and my last strand

of self-worth

as the string.

Why can't your tears just sew me up
instead?

There's enough of them here,

just look on the ground.

We are not going to the hospital.

We can use your tears instead.

I didn't mean it,

I was just lonely.

I'm just dumb.

It's not you,

It's not him,

It's not her,

It's not them.

I can't handle

my emotions sometimes

and they overflow.

I didn't mean it.

P  l e a s e.

Don't take me

back there,

*please*

I didn't mean it.

I shouldn't have done it,

I don't even remember doing it.

I'm sorry,

I didn't mean it.

It won't happen again,

I promise.

Please.

*What*

*Have*

*I*

*Done*

*?*

Pulling the bandage off

was my least favorite part.

I shook so violently,

it caused an earthquake in my hospital bed.

From the hospital bed to the floor,

The floor to the chair you were sitting in,

From your chair

right to those beautiful eyes of yours.

I shook so hard,

I shook the tears right out of you.


*-the actual worst part*

Purgatory is just

as brutal

as the initial suffering,

 just quieter.


*-nine stiches later*

I need to open

the nonexistent windows

and wash the hospital smell off the
sheets.

I cannot feel this air anymore.


*-terrified*

Her back was turned to me

and in between shakes

and wet eyes she said,

*I don't belong here.*

She said it demandingly.

She said it loud.

The type of loud and demanding,

like she wasn't sure

if she was trying to convince,

Me,

Herself Or

the doctor down the hall.

My sobs told her

I didn't belong here either.

They got more violent when she told me

she had been here for four days.

My visit isn't going to take three hours

like the nurse at the hospital told me.

I am going to stay here...

Too crazy to live in my own house

And too reckless

to have the drawstring left in my sweat pants,

 I am stuck here.

And I have no one to blame

but myself.

Warm OJ,

tar-like coffee

and undercooked noodles

in salty brown water.

White walls and professionals

who look like they're taking pity

on a homeless puppy.

You can take

the telephone wires out of my room

and my shoelaces out of my boots,

but this is no way

to mend me back together.


*-mental health facilities are a joke*

I can feel myself

trying to bust free

of this rotting smell

and the wall of curtains

that are surprisingly whiter than my
sheets.

Sobs and whimpers,

Fist fights and shrieks,

The sound of other people's demons

slice through my ears

and the 4am silence

just the same.

Lonely,

but not alone.

How terrifying.

I would search the earth

10 times over

to be set free

of this melancholy.

I could see it in your eyes.

You realized enough was enough,

when you stopped hearing about the
pain

and saw it instead.

*-slit wrist scars*

I took your advice.

I figured since she put me here,

she'd want to help me stay here.

She left three days early.


*-I am on my own*

# The
# Blossoms

No one is coming to save me.

*-start fighting like it*

Inhale love,

Exhale hate.

*-5 am meditation thoughts*

Whatever you are searching

so desperately for,

it cannot be found buried

three inches between my legs.


*-I am not your Band-Aid*

She was

the rain water

that came when I needed it most.

She cleaned the dirt off my stems and
petals,

She gave me enough life

to bloom.

Today,

The weight of it all

seems too much.

That's ok,

I can try again tomorrow.

There were days I cried
because I was expected.
Days when I cried,
because everyone else around me was
crying
too.
And there were days
I was left alone because people
*could tell* I needed my space.
That part wasn't real.
What was real came four months later.
It punched me in the stomach
as I lay gasping for air
on my closet floor.
It was the type of pain
no kindness could cure.
No embrace.
No words.
Nobody in this entire world.

Nothing could give me back

the piece of my heart

that died when you did.


-you can give it back to me in our next
life

You crucify your

needs and wants

in the name of calling yourself

the messiah.

You let Judas

lie and steal and laugh

just so you can bleed for him,

because bleeding for him

is easier than letting him go.


*-stop bleeding, let him go*

I wish

I could stop thinking

with my heart.

But what a magical thing that is,

to live and think in the moment.

There are people

who spend their whole life

trying to plan every second of every day

and we all end up in the same place

when it's all over.

I wish I was smart enough

to not think with my heart,

But I don't want to lose my magic.

I will forever look
and not find you.
I will never find you,
So, I should not look.


*-scanning a crowd three years later*

Above the anger,

The selfish choices you made

And above the passion,

I'm just a hurt woman

who longs for someone

I would never let myself have again


*-it hurts but I've learned and I'm happy
on my own*

Things always come

in threes.

Even the truth.


*-my truth, your truth, the real truth*

I hope she admires
your compassion
the way I did.
I hope all the parts
I loved about you
are still there.

*-best case scenario*

Looking into her eyes

felt like those few seconds of silence

on the freeway

in a rainstorm

as you pass under a bridge.

So unexpected

So peaceful.

Being with her,

my soul could just breathe for a second.

*-my water and my wine*

I have stood up

and walked out of quicksand

with sea anchors tied to each shoulder.

If you leave,

it is simply a few less pounds.

I will be just fine.

I just wanted to digest fire with her.

It could inch down my throat,

burn by burn

and destroy

every part of my world,

But if I was with her,

it was worth it.

Do you think

they ever look back and think,

*Wow*

*How lucky was I*

*to have shared a life with her,*

*even if only for a split second?*

You are not the only one

who has something to lose;

Look around you.

They have their monsters just like you.

I'd bet anything,

they need someone to listen,

just like you did.


*-don't let your friends think they're alone*

Working on loving yourself

can be challenging.

I get better at it day by day.

There is a list from here to the moon

of things

I shouldn't be able to love about myself,

but I do.

With one exception.

You

make me realize,

I still have work to do.

Having similar scars

is only scary,

because we all take care of them

a little differently.

I don't want to bloom gracefully.

I want to bloom

unapologetically,

Abrasive and passionate.

I yearn to bloom

demandingly.


*-like a weed I think*

How could someone
be so self-centered
as to think another
person cannot go on
without them?

No longer will

I cater

to a delicate sense

of masculinity.

I will burn this man's world to the
ground.


*-a vow*

Realizing why my parents

did what they did is terrifying.

What if I must make those choices
someday?

I wouldn't be able to do

any better than they have.


*-they are who they are for their own
reasons*

Do not tell me

you are on my side

when you have defended the accused

for so long.

How dare you teach your girls

body shame

and embarrassment,

while your boys are basked

in diluted consequences

and vile encouragement.

I am on my own in this world,

Your justice is not my justice

And I will no longer let you tell me

it is.


*-I alone am responsible for my own justice*

He's kind of her savior in a way.

She's constantly leaving scars and bruises

on everything she touches,

But he's always there to help her heal.

*-Father time and Mother Nature*

Youth is free,

Wisdom is costly.


-respect your elders

I always found them odd,

Men who praise women for loving
blindly.

The type of women

who love as hard as they can,

only to get back unattainable
expectations

and the empty ribcage of a heartless
lover.

It's like,

men fear women on a pedestal

All because if they can look each other

at eye level,

Then they are equals.

How fragile masculinity can be and

how sad I am

for the women who love as hard as they
can

without getting love in return.

*-do not love blindly, love selfishly*

There is only

so much oxygen

in the world designated to me.

Stop taking it all up.


*-you're the worst*

The rape split you open

Not in half.

Things will get better,

I promise.

When I was younger,

no wasn't an option.

It was beat out of my vocabulary at the
age of 13

by a spoiled man who was so used to
hearing yes,

he couldn't control himself if he heard
anything else.

These days,

I have mastered it perfectly and you can
too.

Say it over and over again

when combing your hair in the morning

and when brushing your teeth before
bed.

Practice it

when a strange man asks for your
number.

Or when you don't want to go on just
one first date.

Practice no if his hand is too far up your
leg

and practice it when it seems to be the
scariest choice of words.

Be strong in it.

Make it comfortable for you.

We live in a world where the word no
shouldn't be public knowledge.

We live in a world where masculinity is
caressed,

and male privilege runs more rampant

than female rights.

If you want to

say no,

Say no.

Say no.

Say no.


*-you don't owe anyone anything*

*Dear My Body,*

It wasn't you I was trying to kill.  It wasn't you I hated.

It wasn't my skin and bones that I wanted to destroy.

You are beautiful and I'm sorry.

I'm sorry for taking out what I wanted to do to my mind on you;

you didn't deserve it.

I'm sorry for not nourishing you,

for starving you, for purging you.

I am sorry

for not caring for you the way I should have.

There's not a single thing I would change about the sanctuary of a home you have given me.

Not my skin tone, not how short I am, not how my left brow arches higher than the right.

You have done your job and done it well.

You've kept my soul safe and sound, recovered from every broken bone and held me tighter than any other person ever could.

You have been great to me,

strong for me

and resilient with me.

Thank you.

And I'm sorry.

*Love,*

*The woman who wanted to destroy her demons not her body*

There was too much death

and not enough flowers.

He made me neglect my garden

all winter

and here I am,

Left with only fallen petals

and brown stems.


*-My soul needs spring cleaning too*

Wow.

After all those sunsets,

I still try to remember what he smells
like

at the end of a long day.


-*still working on it*

He left like he had somewhere to be,

so sudden and so fast.

I left like I should have never been there

in the first place,

frantic and apologetically.

I just hope he made it safe and sound.

*-I turned out alright after all this, I hope
you did too*

How naïve

of me to think that just because

she gave me birth,

her problems

wouldn't become

mine someday.

Just because my soul

falls to its knees

hoping you'll come back

doesn't mean you're wanted here.

To accept inequality

is an injustice to your sisters.

Do not let them get away with it.

Hold them responsible.

Let them know what they have done,

And feel proud when they do not do it
again.


*-you are responsible for your own
equality*

Her roots were nourished in soil

drenched in her father's tears.

Her stems sprouted with the strength

her mother had at the age of 18

when she realized

the grandmother of her unborn twins

drove her to an abortion clinic

instead of church.

She was capable of such wonderful
things,

she was the brightest flower

in every garden she graced.

She was the type of flower

a painter could sit in front of for hours

but never get it just quite right.

And it didn't matter how long they sat
there,

they'd never be able to replicate

her passion for understanding

or her absolute radiating lust for life.

Lucky for me,

she's not a flower

and I'm not a painter.


*-my flower*

There is a strange type of sisterhood

in being the same kind

of gentle fool

who fell

for the same selfish lies.


*-I can never stop wondering if she's
healing at the same speed I am*

There are lines

that should not

and will not be crossed.

Let me highlight them in yellow for you,

since you forgot your glasses.


*-step back and sit down*

Who wants to listen to bombs explode
and cities disintegrate
when I can listen to the silence
of my truth instead?


*-it takes two*

I want equality,

not revenge.


*-men mustn't realize how lucky they are*

In the long run,

he forgave me.

Or at least he's working on it.


*-pops*

I will no longer

let people dismantle me

for their diluted sense of satisfaction.


*-you shouldn't either*

There is such beautiful strength

in people

who have accepted apologies

they've never received.

Do you realize how challenging that is?

If I wasn't afraid,

Nothing would excite me.

*-cheap thrills*

We say we won't be like our parents,

but their problems will land in your lap

just the way they landed in their parents
before them.

My knees will buckle nervously

the way my mother's did

when she found out she was having a
child

and my left brow will sweat

just the way my father's always does

on a summer day.

I'll face the same trials of deceit and
betrayal

as insecurity and mental illness

hover over me like

the ghost of our family's past.

My problems are my grandparents

and their problems were their
grandparents.

But I have the tools I need to be happy.

I can do this.


*-a dysfunctional family doesn't mean a dysfunctional life*

There are days I wake up
and I am thankful.
Enough days have finally passed
for time to heal all wounds.
And there are days I wake up
yearning for a time machine,
to launch myself forward
to a day when yesterday
wasn't in my nightmares.

As a woman,

on certain days

there's

No Places

For Kindness.

I read somewhere

that we are all made of stardust.

If stars are in the sky and in me,

then I'm never truly alone.

I am surrounded by the brightest parts of
me

every night while they remind me,

I am enough to light up my own world.

Do not

argue with me

about feminism.

Misogyny has been imbedded into

you since you were inside of your
mother.

Your god has a gender,

How blind

can you be?

I am not a rehabilitation institution.

If you are not whole yet,

I cannot fix you.

Come back to me

when you have finished the work,

you need to do.


*-I'll be right here*

Power tastes good,

but nothing tastes better than happiness.

And there are people so hurt
themselves,

it exudes out of every orifice.

They must make everyone around

them feel the pain they're in.

People who play with power like that

will never be truly happy.

But you will.

And that's why

you'll always win in these situations.

You'll win,

don't worry, baby.

Trusting

Is

Not

A

sin.

And

I

Will

no

longer

let

him

make

me

think

it

is.

Brick by brick

I can deconstruct the walls

I've taken years to build.

The world deserves to see my heart,

and my heart deserves to see the world.

I can work all day and night

with a smile on my face

and cuts on my knuckles,

But in the morning

when my walls have been torn down,

and my face can finally look up at the
sun,

I will know,

all the strength

needed to knock down my walls

was right here the whole time.

I told her that one day

she would wake up, in her own bed,

surrounded by photos of her and her
friends.

She'll slip out of the baby blue and grey
sheets

she picked out

and she'll walk into the kitchen

she decided would be country chic.

And after she made her coffee,

she could sit on her patio

and watch the world around her go by.

Maybe for a split second

she'll remember

how empty and how broken she was

lying in a white room with a stranger,

crying loud enough for the whole world
to hear.

And for every moment after that,

She could sip her coffee,

with her head a little higher

and her heart a little more peaceful

knowing she had finally fixed her heart,

all on her own.

*-I hope her day comes soon, too*

When I stopped pouring my sunlight

into him

and started pouring it into my own soul,

my world lit up before my very eyes.

I learned through trial and error,

if I am my truest self,

love will beam into my windows

and caress life back into me.

There can be light in my world,

if I simply let it shine in the right places.


*-redirect*

Happy air

has a different smell.

It hangs in the air

Just to let you know,

You're allowed to live freely


*-chamomile, hope and eucalyptus*

Being damaged

is not an excuse to sit on the sidelines

and watch life go on without you.

It is not an excuse

to spend 17 hours a day in bed

and it is not an excuse

to scream the word

*liar*

when

he tells you

he wants to stay.

Being damaged is not an excuse

for living a mediocre life.

Love is real.

So is happiness.

But lust is real too.

Just like greed

And just like selfishness.

And just because my happiness

and my love

Still fight battles of the past,

doesn't mean I have lost.

There is no room in my soul

left for false humility or inflated
affirmation.

Do not waste my time with your fancy
words

and slicked hair.

I haven't the patience.

One day

I will pull my spine out of my mouth

and lay it in front of you.

I'll go vertebrae by vertebrae

explaining why at 22 the doctor told me

my back is degenerating

at the age of a 55-year-old.

But until then,

 my spine is this book,

the pages are the weight I bare.

Every pinched nerve,

And bulging disk Is a part

of who I am.

My future lies in the truth of curiosity.

And if curiosity killed the cat,

Satisfaction brought it back.

How could I not be curious?

After all,

Every single one of us

Is searching for satisfaction somewhere.

On my last day,

I hope whatever put me here

can look me in the deepest parts of my
heart,

Smile,

And know I used

every drop of

love,

talent

and compassion.

I don't want there to be a single drop
left.

I want to give all of myself to this world.

It is not easy,

But you are capable of happiness,

I have seen it in you.

Do not hold yourself back.

May peace find

that beautiful soul of yours,

It's the least you deserve.

Between these pages lies the heart and soul of my struggles. Most of this book was written while feverishly typing under the table during afternoon happy hour and drunkenly laid out flat in the back seat of an uber at three am. Though my days are currently drenched in love and hope, there was a time when these words were so heavy in my heart, I couldn't focus on anything else. I had to get them out somewhere. I'm honestly not even sure if this is poetry, just things that are too deep for twitter and too loud to stay in my head. Since writing this book, I have felt so relieved. I've gone back and forth about my choice to publish this for months, but my final decision is to do it. I refuse to let something as insignificant as my own silly fears stand in my way at this point. There are 7 billion people in this world, I'm not the only one to feel these things. But I have gone through phases where I thought I was, and I don't want others to feel that way. This is my journey, this is my story and though the ending may not be the happy, satisfying or fulfilling ending you're looking for, my story is still unfolding. Each day I get closer and closer to true happiness and one day it'll ooze into my work just as the hurt has. But for today, here it is. May this book let you know, you are never alone, and you possess everything needed to live the life you deserve.

*special acknowledgments*

1. *Jared* for believing in me even when I didn't.

2. *Lauren* for being as passionate about this book as I've been, since day one. I am so lucky to know you, Lauren. Thank you, a million times!

3. *Erica, Tiffany, Juan and Dana* for sacrificing time and helping me make this book the best is can be.

4. *Torri* for drawing the cover of this book.

4. *Alcohol* for, you know...everything.

292

As an aspiring actor, model, dancer and author, *Alexis Marie* is constantly  looking for new and creative forms of expression. Though she is continuously growing and recreating herself, she spends most of her time working as a full time performer for one of the largest entertainment companies in the world and loves every second. As she continues her quest to take over the world, she has realized just how important self-care and self-expression can be. She can be found keeping up with her ambitious projects and adventurous way of living through her social media.

Instagram: @AuthorAlexisMarie

69222618R00163

Made in the USA
Columbia, SC
14 August 2019